AN IMPORTANT NOTE FROM THE AUTHOR

This book is not a substitute for good common sense. If you find yourself charged with a serious offense, you should seek the advice of a skilled attorney.

However, if you are charged with a minor violation or infraction, this book can be invaluable to you in preparing your own defense. The author assumes no responsibility for the ultimate decision of any court you appear before.

TRAFFIC TICKETS, FINES, AND OTHER ANNOYING THINGS

BY
TIM MATHESON

Editor — Mike Konz

CITADEL PRESS   SECAUCUS, NEW JERSEY

Special thanks to my wife Karen, daughters Dawn, Debbie, Sondi, Jennie and son Timmy II, with special thanks to my mom, Jean and Mrs. Kay McCumber.

Published 1984 by Citadel Press
A division of Lyle Stuart Inc.
120 Enterprise Avenue, Secaucus, N.J. 07094
In Canada: Musson Book Company
A division of General Publishing Co. Limited
Don Mills, Ontario

Copyright © 1982 by T & K Publishers
318 14th Street, Sidney, Nebraska

All rights reserved. No part of this book
may be reproduced in any form, except by
a newspaper or magazine reviewer who wishes
to quote brief passages in connection
with a review.

Queries regarding rights and permissions should be
addressed to: Lyle Stuart Inc., 120 Enterprise Avenue,
Secaucus, N.J. 07094

Manufactured in the United States of America

ISBN 0-8065-0883-3

TABLE OF CONTENTS

CHAPTER		PAGE
1.	Your Driver's License and How to Keep It	5
2.	Common Sense Driving Techniques	7
	Interstate Highways	8
	Speed Enforcement by Aircraft	8
	State Highways	10
	Driving on City Streets	11
	Speed Traps	12
	Bond Cards	13
3.	Radar (Its Care and Feeding)	14
	What Is Radar?	14
	Is Radar Reliable?	14
	Do Radar Operators Make Mistakes?	15
	How Good Is Radar?	15
	Can Police Radar Be Jammed?	15
	Problems with Radar	16
	Batching Effect	16
	Scanning	16
	Panning Effect	17
	Shadow Effect	17
	Ads Errors	17
	Averaging	18
	PLL	18
	Target Misidentifications	18
	Heater Defroster Fans	19
	Radar Case Law	20
	Summary	20
4.	Busted or Not (It's Up to You)	21
	What Should I Say?	21
	Roadside Manner	22
	Should I Try to Talk My Way Out of a Ticket?	23
	Should I Try to Intimidate the Officer?	24
	Vascar Reading?	24
	What's Taking So Long?	24
	Driver Forgot His/Her Driver's License	24
	Does Not Have the Registration or Proof of Ownership for the Car He/She Is Driving	25
	Checking You for a Wanted Person	25
5.	Preparing Yourself for Court (Without an Attorney)	26
	Speeding	26
	Stop Signs	27
	Driving Left of Center	27
	Following Too Close	28
	Red Lights, Turn Arrows, No Turn Signs	28

TABLE OF CONTENTS

CHAPTER		PAGE
	The Officer Preparing for Trial	29
	What Does the Prosecutor Have to Prove?	30
	Initial Appearance	31
	Continuance	31
	Trial Date	32
	Basic Speed Rules	33
	Duty Upon Approaching Stop Sign	33
	The Judge's Opening Remarks	34
	Motion to Amend a Citation (Ticket)	34
	The State's Case	35
	Direct Testimony	35
	Cross Examination	35
	Re-Direct Testimony	35
	Your Motion for a Directed Verdict of Not Guilty	35
	Prosecutor Failed to Establish Foundation for Testimony	36
	Defendant's Case	36
	Your Turn to Testify	36
	What Should You Do on the Witness Stand?	37
	Resting Your Case	37
	Recalling a Witness	37
	Closing Arguments	37
	The Verdict	38
	What Can I Do If I'm Found Guilty?	38
	Summary	39
6.	Defendant's Guide to the Prosecutor's Case	40
	How to Use This Guide	40
	Physical Evidence Outline Guide	41
	Speeding Mobile Radar Outline Guide	43
	Speeding Vascar Outline Guide	46
	Speed (Aircraft Clock) Outline	49
	Following Too Close Outline	54
	Stop Sign Violations Outline	55
	Red Light Violations Outline	57
	Other Minor Violations Outline	59
	Glossary of Legal Terms	61

CHAPTER ONE
YOUR DRIVER'S LICENSE AND HOW TO KEEP IT

Driving today is more a must than a luxury. Commuting by an automobile is necessary. Without rapid movement from place to place opportunities would pass us by. This ability to move rapidly from place to place hinges most singularly upon your ability to keep your license to drive. This book is designed to show you how to keep that most important permit.

This book will not touch on serious traffic violations, but focus on minor offenses. These minor offenses left unattended or uncontested will lead to the loss of your license. Beyond the loss of that privilege it can lead to disaster to your checkbook, job security, and your very livelihood. Believe for a moment you could not drive legally to work every day fearing arrest at any moment for driving under suspension. Imagine you must depend on a friend, relative or perhaps rapid transit to get from place to place. Some could live with that, but I couldn't.

I have written this book as a common-sense guide to keeping your license to drive. The system as mysterious as you see it now would have you believe the only way to fight a ticket is hiring an attorney. Let's face it, most of us can't and won't hire a high priced legal source to defend us in a minor traffic offense. It's easier to just pay the fine and be done with it, even if you believed you were innocent. YOU may not realize the simple act of pleading guilty, paying your fine and losing points can and usually does have far-reaching effects, the least of which is your immediate loss of money; the most dramatic is the suspension of your license.

Between these extremes is one simple fact: Convictions of traffic offenses will cost you money. And a lot of it. Where, you ask? I paid my fine. That should be the end of it. Shouldn't it???

Not on your life. When insurance companies get word of the violation, your rates go up, up, up. How much your premium increases depends on your driving record. The worse your driving record, the more it will cost your pocket. Those rates go up even if you were *innocent*, but went and paid your fine. Insurance companies only look at traffic convictions and accidents. *These* factors determine the premium you pay, not whether you thought you were innocent of the violation.

Keeping your license is your responsibility. If you don't care, rest assured that no one else will. Your license and keeping it depends on how you protect it. This book will not explain any illegal way to avoid a conviction or citation. It will describe certain legal techniques you can use to avoid citations and convictions. These are the "nuts and bolts" of what it takes to keep your license.

JUST WHAT DOES IT TAKE TO KEEP YOUR LICENSE?

I have been kidded by police officers and others that all I need to tell the readers is to be sure to obey every law all the time. A great resolution. But like many resolutions it's an impossible dream, unless a computer is driving your vehicle.

"We are only human" applies so well here. We all make mistakes. It's difficult to pay 100% attention to our driving all the time and stay within the speed limit. We don't intend to speed, we simply were careless for a moment. Unfortunately, the lack of *intent* has nothing to do with proof of guilt. Unlike criminal offenses, the State has no obligation to establish intent. Though you did not intend to speed, run a stop sign, etc., the court could find you guilty.

The mere fact you were speeding is sufficient to convict you.

Protecting your license to drive MUST START with the very first citation, NOT when you are within a few points of losing it and dealing with high risk insurance companies.

Or worse yet, **WALKING**!!!

What qualifies me to write this book? I make no claim to being an expert. "Expert" has been defined as anyone fifty miles from home wearing a suit and carrying a briefcase. What I have seen, heard and learned qualifies me to write this book. I am a veteran police officer who specializes in traffic enforcement.

In that capacity, I have written many citations. After writing those citations, I have spent countless hours in traffic court as a prosecution witness.

With very *few* exceptions, I rarely had the opportunity to witness a defendant properly present his or her case. I honestly believe some of those who appeared thought they were innocent, but so badly managed their defense that the judge had no alternative but to find them guilty. I have made every effort to prepare the average person to properly defend himself in court, or avoid citations altogther. I am confident this book will be of great value to you.

CHAPTER TWO
COMMON-SENSE DRIVING TECHNIQUES

Occasionally most of us must have our memory jogged about our driving habits. This chapter is devoted to pointing out and refreshing our memory of driving techniques that, if constantly violated, will almost assure contact by police. Generally, this will mean some type of enforcement action. Enforcement action comes in three forms: Verbal warning, written warning, and written citation.

In any event, being stopped is time-consuming, inconvenient, and occasionally costly beyond simply the fine and court costs, the points assessed your license and rocketing insurance costs.

In some cases, insurance costs can triple. I spoke with an insurance agent who has seen cases of drivers being charged $1,200 to $1,800 a year on assigned risk policies as the result of poor driving habits.

Driving techniques will vary depending on location. These locations can generally be broken down into four main areas:

Interstate
State Highways
County Roads
City Streets

Each of these will be examined in depth.

Interstate Highway

Sometimes referred to as the "super slab" and generally patrolled by State Police, State Troopers or Highway Patrolmen, all of whom are "affectionately" referred to as "Bears." This four-lane super highway stretches from state to state, coast to coast, and border to border, a godsend to rapid movement of traffic, merchandise, produce, and all manner of Interstate Commerce. That is, it was open to rapid movement until the federal government imposed a 55 mph speed limit, which it implemented by threatening state governments with withdrawal of Federal Highway funds if compliance wasn't assured.

That's all history. We're now required to comply with a 55 mph speed limit on these highways.

Bearing that in mind, a few common-sense driving techniques may save you unpleasant contact with police.

The most obvious is to travel at 55 so you won't be stopped for speeding. But at 55, you will have your doors blown off by other motorists and run the risk of being rear-ended by an impatient, inattentive motorist.

Common-sense driving techniques dictate that there are some things you can do to reduce your chances of police contact because of your driving habits. If you insist on frequent lane changes, passing everything in sight, speeding up and slowing down frequently for no apparent reason, your risk of having a law enforcement officer's attention focus on you is greatly increased. If his attention focuses your way and you are in violation of a law, a citation could be the result.

When driving the Interstate System, the interchanges can be the most active for law enforcement. However, be aware that white marks, whether they be blocks, rectangles, or silhouettes of airplanes, and usually placed one mile apart, indicate aircraft may be checking your speed.

Speed Enforcement by Aircraft

It is a scientific fact that an object (in this case, a car, truck, semi-trailer) going from Point A (a white mark on the highway) to Point B (the second white mark on the highway) must maintain velocity. The time it takes to travel from mark to mark is a measure of that velocity. If the white marks (which will be large enough to be seen from the air) are exactly 5,280 feet apart (one statute mile) and an object travels that distance in 60 seconds (one minute), the vehicle is traveling 60 m.p.h.

If the vehicle travels the distance in 65 seconds, the speed of that vehicle is 55 mph.

Operators inside these aircraft have good visibility and can see your car from great range. Ten miles from clocking point to citation is not uncommon.

Numerous "test" cases have upheld the validity of this type of enforcement by stating in brief that a police officer may, in the enforcement of the law, use the totality of his experience and information obtained from other law enforcement officers and reliable sources.

officer in an aircraft when the aircraft officer advises the ground officer that a particular vehicle is violating the law. Based upon that belief, the ground officer can issue a citation or other enforcement action as deemed appropriate. Usually when aircraft are being used, citations are the rule and warnings the exception.

When the case goes to court, both the ground officer and the air officer must be present if the ground officer is basing the complaint upon the air officer's observation. The ground officer will testify as to the driver's identification and the air officer will testify as to the actual violation.

Summary of Interstate Driving

Driving the interstate can be very boring and sometimes hypnotic. Be alert to this situation and change drivers every several hundred miles. Use rest stops. Time yourself between mile markers and check the accuracy of your speedometer.

Speed should be reasonable and prudent for existing conditions. It would not be prudent to drive 55 (the posted maximum) on an icy road, in driving rain, snow, dust or any time visibility is severely reduced. On the other hand, if you find yourself in rush hour traffic in a major city and all the traffic is traveling 65, the odds of your being stopped for speeding at 65 are practically non-existent. However, if your speed was excessive and you were passing every one in sight, your odds of being caught are greatly increased.

The law requires you to follow the vehicle in front of you at a safe and reasonable distance. Some traffic safety persons recommend two seconds for each ten miles per hours of speed. That theory works fine for country driving. But leave a space like that between your car and the one you are following on a major freeway or highway during rush hour and your fellow motorists will gladly fill the open space, leaving you no choice but to follow along.

If, however, traffic is light and well spaced except for your car, which is unreasonably close to the rear bumper of the car in front of you, being stopped for following too close is a real possibility. If you hit someone from the rear, most jurisdictions will find the fault with you.

Lane changes must be made safely and signaled before the change in lanes is made. Frequent and unsignaled lane changes are received very poorly by most law enforcement officers.

Passing everything and everyone in sight is an invitation to police contact. If you are passing everyone you come upon, it is likely that you are speeding. Obviously there is a reason for their reduced speed.

Be especially alert for the tell-tale aircraft markers on the highway. There is very little compromise on the part of the ground officer when he stops you based on an air craft officer's observation of your vehicle's speed.

It is important to carry your license and registration in your car or on your person. A registration certificate is NOT your certificate of title. A registration certificate is given to you when you pay your tax on the vehicle and buy your license plates. It must be carried in your vehicle to prove who owns the car.

Your title should never be carried in your vehicle. If your car is stolen, that title could be the means for someone to sell your vehicle by forging your name.

State Highways

The same rules of common-sense driving that apply to state highways apply to Interstate or toll roads (turnpikes), only there are more of them. State highways are in most places only two lane roadways which, of course, means a multitude of passing restrictions:

No passing zones
Yellow lines
Double yellow lines
Passing in the face of oncoming traffic
Passing in an intersection
Passing on the crest of a hill
Passing on the right
Passing on the left

If you apply a little common sense, you can avoid police contact. No passing zones are commonly marked by a triangle-shaped sign cleverly worded "No passing" and a yellow solid line on your side of the highway. Most people don't know that all passing must be completed before you reach the solid yellow line. Failure to do so may result in citation.

Driving on City Streets

The average motorist does most of his driving on city streets. It is on city streets that the majority of property damage accidents occur. Therefore, the odds of police contact on city streets is extremely high. Most city police officers are charged with strict enforcement of traffic, especially in certain areas, such as:

- School zones when children are in attendance
- School bus stops
- High accident areas
- Areas where special hazards exist such as construction sites, poorly engineered areas, etc.

Be aware that motorcycle police officers are primarily charged with traffic law enforcement. However, don't ignore the "beat" car.

The same basics that apply to freeway, interstate or turnpike driving apply to city streets. There are, however, several other tips that should be considered.

School Zones

School zones are watched very closely. No one wants a problem in a school zone. Some jurisdictions have doubled the fines that are assessed against a guilty motorist for a violation in a school zone. Be aware of special restrictions in these areas.

Some jurisdictions prohibit the passing of one vehicle by another in a school zone. This includes a four, five, or multi-lane bidirection roadway. I have seen many drivers stopped for this violation honestly unaware the violation occurred.

Some jurisdictions require motorists to stop and remain stopped until the school zone crosswalk is completely empty.

There, again, you can find yourself in legal trouble without being aware that you are violating a law.

Common-sense driving indicates "When in Rome, do as the Romans." What I want to get across to you is this: If you find yourself in an unfamiliar area, imitate the way the majority of motorists are driving, and avoid a citation.

Bear in mind that city police officers deal more with crime than traffic offenses per se. However, traffic stops based on a real violation of the law (face it, there are hundreds of laws we can and do violate) have produced information leading to the arrest of many violators of more serious laws.

Remember, police officers are trained observers. Therefore, if something catches their eye and is any way suspicious or illegal, the odds of being stopped are greatly increased.

I am telling you this so you may have a better understanding of why an officer may stop you for what you would consider a nit-picking violation. Be polite and courteous, and you will most likely be rewarded with a warning.

Inattention or confusion account for the majority of traffic accidents and citations. Generally speaking, speeding, rolling a stop sign, failure to signal your turns, etc., alone do not cause accidents, unless, of course, the violation is excessive.

However, if you compound the violation with either inattention or confusion, you have an accident looking for a place to happen. Not only that, but your odds of being stopped and cited are greatly increased.

Inattentive driving is so hazardous that I usually will cite for it even on the smallest violation. You can't be paying attention to your driving if you have your head turned and are talking with your passenger.

City Streets, County Roads, State Highways and Speed Traps

I want to spend just a little more time on speed traps. For those of you who don't know what a speed trap is, I will give you a definition.

Speed Trap: An area where law enforcement's efforts in reducing speed or requiring compliance with the speed law is heavily concentrated. Law enforcement vehicles may conceal themselves, use a radar unit and work in pairs. The hidden police car clocks you and radios your speed to a chase car. Citations are usually the result of this police contact.

I am familiar with a town that has approximately three miles of state highway. It is not uncommon for them to have an officer at each end of the town. It is also common to have a motorist stopped at one end of town for speeding and stopped again for speeding at the other end of town. You can be cited for as many violations as you commit.

How do you spot a speed trap? You can't, until you find

yourself caught in one. That is, unless the trusty old C.B. warns you of what's ahead.

When you approach a community, common sense advises that you comply with its speed laws and all its other laws. Be especially watchful around small towns. Those communities don't want traffic whizzing through town, endangering citizens.

Once again, the old inattention/confusion factor gets more people stopped than deliberately speeding through a town or city. Use common sense and save your hard-earned money.

Bond Cards

I strongly recommend to any motorist who travels state to state with any regularity to obtain a bond card from a noted auto club. Bond cards are honored in most states and will save you from posting a hefty dollar bond to secure your release from custody. Bond cards are NOT honored if you are charged with an alcohol related violation.

CHAPTER THREE
RADAR
(Its Care and Feeding)

A certain mystique surrounds the pulsing workings of radar. This highly accurate electronics device, when used properly, will tell the operator within one mile an hour (plus or minus) the speed of a baseball pitched by the star pitcher, the velocity reading of a football, and the speed of a motor vehicle.

Since your reason for reading this book is concern for your license and wallet, we'll focus on the latter of the examples — speed of a motor vehicle.

Radar comes in many shapes and sizes. It has been around for a long time, and like most devices that stick around, has become better with age. I hope in this chapter to dispel the mystique and explain the reality.

Police traffic radar feeds when you exceed the speed limit. The more times you speed, the more you feed the radar with your money and points.

Is it possible to defeat such a contraption? Possibly, if you have a basic working knowledge of what radar is.

Radar, you will soon find, is nothing more than a tool and only as good or bad as the person operating it. If the person using the equipment knows little of its use and operation, the equipment is compromised and the outcome is of very little value.

WHAT IS RADAR?

Radar is an acronym. It is an abbreviation for Radio Detection and Ranging. That's nice, but what does it mean? Basically, police traffic radar is a piece of electronic equipment designed to calculate the velocity (speed) of a motor vehicle. It accomplishes its task by sending a signal from the antenna of the radar. The equipment then measures how long it takes for the signal to return. The radar then computes the information into a speed reading. Radar will function in both mobile or stationary situations, depending on the design, and how it is used.

IS RADAR RELIABLE?

Is it reliable? Can its readings be trusted? Radar units themselves are finely constructed pieces of electronic equipment. Unbiased scientific tests have shown consistently that radar instruments used in traffic enforcement are reliable and effective tools when carefully used and properly maintained. It has to be pointed out that radar is only a tool manufactured, designed and built to be as accurate and reliable as scientifically possible. Does radar make mistakes? Generally and practically speaking, no.

DO RADAR OPERATORS MAKE MISTAKES?

The answer to that question, of course, is yes; and some of them make many mistakes. Human error has been the route of almost all successful challenges to radar.

As a good case in point, in Dade County, Florida, the rumor spread rapidly that radar would detect trees traveling 85 m.p.h., 28 m.p.h. houses, and cars traveling much faster than they actually were. All the Dade County cases showed that when certain basic operating procedures were violated, these kinds of absurd speed measurements did occur. If the operator doesn't know or care what he's doing, he can foul up. The evidence his radar produces will be worthless.

JUST HOW GOOD IS RADAR?

It is only as good as the operator. If he is competent, radar readings will be valid, accurate, and, in most states and jurisdictions, will be accepted as prima facie evidence (on the surface without having to prove anything else.)

CAN POLICE RADAR BE JAMMED?

Jamming a police radar by electronic means is illegal. If you are detected with a jamming device, you'll not only be treading on F.C.C. regulations, but face possible charges in a jurisdiction with laws against interfering with police radio or radar.

Other methods are not illegal. I'll give a few examples of some ridiculous "legal" techniques that have been suggested for jamming police radars.

Trim strips of metal foil placed on the car's body are thought by many to be a way to trick radar. It's ridiculous, really. The metal strips will only increase the ability of your vehicle to reflect the radar beam and make it an easier target.

Hanging chains attached to the underside of your vehicle is another example how drivers try to fool radar. This might prevent static electricity build-up, but it won't reduce the radar energy reflected.

Some drivers place small metal objects or aluminum strips inside the vehicle's hubcaps. That's a noisy, annoying idea.

— 15 —

PROBLEMS WITH RADAR

Angular or co-sine effect: What does that mean? Reader, that means you have an advantage when the officer is sitting stationary on the side of the road. The greater the angle between the radar and your vehicle, the greater the suspicion of doubt. That doubt is in your favor. The radar would indicate a lower than true speed. Let's say you were traveling 70 m.p.h. and the police radar antennas were 15 degrees to either side of your vehicle. The operator would see a reading on his radar Unit of 67.61 m.p.h.—lower than your true speed. The radar was in error, but in your favor.

BATCHING EFFECT

This is a special problem that affects only mobile radar. It is caused by slight time lags in the moving radar's sensing/computing cycle. This can lead to either lower or higher target speeds depending on the circumstances.

The Batching effect might happen if the patrol car is rapidly accelerated or decelerated while a radar measurement is being obtained. In simple terms, the computer in the radar may not be able to keep up with these drastic speed changes. Suppose the patrol car was rapidly accelerating. The radar would indicate a higher than true speed reading of the target vehicle. The exact opposite would be true if the patrol car was decelerating. The target vehicle's speed would be lower than a true reading. When this occurs, the officer can solve the problem by trying to maintain a fairly constant patrol speed to obtain an enforceable reading. If the batching effect occurred the radar was wrong: therefore a reasonable doubt may exist.

SCANNING

This so-called error exists from the theoretical possibility that when a radar beam is moved rapidly across a flat plane, the plane moves closer. For example, a hand-held radar might be swung swiftly past the side of a parked car, brick wall, or some other stationary object, and a speed measurement may be produced. What happens, of course, is that swinging the device creates **relative motion** between the radar and the stationary object; therefore, the radar sees a speed reading that is incorrect. Obviously the solution to the problem is for the officer to insure the radar is not being moved from side to side or up or down rapidly.

PANNING EFFECT

This effect happens only to two-piece radar units. If the antenna of the radar were pointed at its own computing module, an erroneous speed measurement might occur. NOTE: You should look at how the radar antenna is positioned in the patrol car and make a note of it.

SHADOW EFFECT

Moving radar may be susceptible to another problem that does not affect stationary radar. Shadow effect is a real problem and can cause higher than true target speeds.

The radar beam that was intended to strike the ground instead strikes a large, moving truck which reflects a stronger signal than the ground. The radar then uses the signal reflected from the truck and lowers the radar's patrol speed indication. Remember, the radar is a computor and as such will compute only the information it receives. If the patrol speed indication on the radar readout is incorrect the target speed indication will also be wrong.

Let's look at a brief example of how this can drastically increase a target vehicle's speed "as the radar sees it."

Suppose the patrol car is traveling at 50 m.p.h. and the large truck at 40 m.p.h. The speed of the patrol car relative to the truck is only 10 m.p.h. In effect, the radar would "think" that the truck is the ground and this ground is moving at 40 m.p.h.

Meanwhile the radar is tracking a target vehicle that is approaching the patrol car. The radar computer goes into action and computes the speed of the target vehicle as 110 m.p.h., much greater than the target's actual speed of 70 m.p.h. The radar operator can detect this error by close monitoring of his patrol speed, but if the operator becomes careless and you were to ask him about his own patrol speed on the witness stand, I wonder what would happen to his speeding case against you.

ADS ERRORS

Anyone who owns a radar detector has been driven nuts on occasion by this function typical of some police radars. The ads switch turns off the radar transmitter, making detectors useless. The ads switch leaves the rest of the radar operating on standby. The ads error as claimed by the manufacturers of radar detectors simply states that when the transmitter is switched on after standby, it will produce a higher than true reading. This may have been true when applied to some of the older tube-type radars, but not of new micro computer radars.

These new radars have special circuits which prohibit reading any signal the unit receives until the target's tracking history is obtained and verified as a Doppler signal rather than electrical noise. A careful radar operator can disprove this error by showing the initial speed indication by the radar was consistent with the later readings and his visual observation of the vehicle's estimated speed.

AVERAGING

This "error" is similar to the alleged ads error. This claim tries to show that the radar could in theory track two vehicles simultaneously, one 40 m.p.h., the other at 60 m.p.h.—compute the average and come up with 50 m.p.h. Circuitry of modern radar makes it impossible to deal with more than one target simultaneously. In reality, if two similiar sized targets are tracked at different speeds, radar will read neither and blank the display. The averaging error does not exist..

PLL

The PLL circuit has made it possible to communicate with craft in distant space and transmit pictures from the moon with uncanny accuracy. It also makes it possible for today's modern radar to track targets with accuracy at greater distances. The Phase Locked Loop is reliable, and there is no PLL error.

BLOWING DUST ERROR

Blowing dust, trees, swinging signs, wind, rain, birds, bats, bugs, snow — none of these affect radar's range or accuracy. Believing they do is pure hogwash.

GHOSTING-REFLECTED SIGNALS

Very dramatic. Also very correct. Modern radar reads ghost signals. However, these signals are so weak a true target such as a truck or car will immediately replace the ghost. The radar, when transmitting, is like a little boy, always looking for something to get into. Being a very sensitive piece of equipment, it will play with any signal it can get. But unlike a little boy, when it gets a real target, it's all business.

TARGET MISIDENTIFICATIONS

To understand this "error" you must use your imagination for a moment. When you are close to a radio, the music is quite loud. Move farther from the radio, and the sound grows weaker.

The same is true for a radar unit. The unit transmits a signal. Farther from the transmitter, the signal becomes dispersed and weak. Remember, the radar not only sends out the signal, but must also receive signal when it "bounces" back (Doppler effect). The radar will then read the first target it comes in contact with, regardless of the size of additional targets. If a reasonable amount of distance exists between two targets — let's say there is twice the distance between your passenger car and semi-truck relative to the radar transmitter — you can bet your car is the target. In order for radar to track the truck and ignore your car, the truck must be 16 times larger than your car. Therefore, if you're running all by yourself with a semi-truck one quarter mile behind you or, at the very least, twice the distance you are from the radar, **you are the target.**

If radar did show target misidentification, it would be the operator's error, not the equipment.

HEATER/DEFROSTER FANS

Radar will read these fans, just as it reads ghost or reflected signals. However, just as it ignores reflected signals, radar also ignores this reading when an actual target is present.

STATIONARY RADAR

Bear in mind, we've only talked about mobile radar.

Stationary radar has very few problems. The only problem stationary radar may have is if the operator has positioned the antenna to transmit through the reading module. How qualified must a police officer be to operate radar?

Courts have little difficulty outlining qualifications for a radar operator. Most jurisdictions qualify officers with knowledge and training to properly set up and read the instrument. It is not required that he understand the scientific principles of radar or be able to explain its internal workings. A few hours of instruction are normally sufficient to qualify an operator.

RADAR CASE LAW

It would be impossible to relate case law for every state. But we have compiled some comments reflecting the basic meaning within the majority of these decisions. As used in this section, "decisions" means the findings of various courts.

Most of these cases consider issues relating to the admissibility and documentation of radar evidence. More specifically, these decisions look at three basic pre-requisites that lead to conviction of a speed violator based on radar information.

THESE FACTORS ARE:

A. Reliability of the radar as a determiner of speed, based upon scientific fact.

B. If the unit actually used was accurate when it was used in each given case.

C. Was the radar in each case properly used by the operator?

The majority of landmark cases on the subject refer to all three areas discussed and expanded as follows:

A. Judicial notice may be taken as to the scientific reliability of radar. (This means the judge can agree radar is valid without testimony from a radar expert.)

B. Judicial notice can be taken upon proof of proper testing that the radar was accurate.

C. The operator of radar is not required to understand the scientific principles of radar. However, the operator must be properly trained in the correct use of radar. This includes setting up the unit, testing for accuracy, and reading it.

D. The bottom line in radar enforcement is: Radar units generally are not in error, though the operator may be in error. Therefore, the focus of your attention should be on the operator, not the radar unit.

Summary: Radar is usually valid. Attention should focus on the operators of radar. However, don't ignore proper procedure in verifying radar as accurate when use preparing your defense.

CHAPTER FOUR
BUSTED OR NOT
(It's Up To You)

Red lights burst in your rear-view mirror. An instant passes and you take that inevitable glance at your speedometer. "Does that cop want me? He's still back there . . . I guess he does."

You slow down and pull to the side of the road. How embarrassing!

"This makes me mad!"

WHAT SHOULD I SAY?

The United States Constitution guarantees every citizen's rights against self-incrimination. No one can force you to be a witness or to testify against yourself. These rights apply not only in a court of law, but also on roadways.

Any time a private citizen is contacted by a member of the public criminal justice system, his rights must not be violated by that member, from the officer on the beat to the judge on the bench.

You have the right to remain silent about the facts surrounding your alleged violation.

You will be required, when accused of a crime, to provide the following information: Who you are, where you live, where you work, date of birth, social security number, physical description, owner of the vehicle you are driving, license plate number, model year of vehicle and vehicle identification number.

Most of this information can be obtained from your driver's license and registration. If for some reason you don't have your driver's license or registration with you, you will still be required to furnish this information. Fail to provide it and you could land in jail.

You are not required to provide the officer with any information about the facts surrounding your alleged violation.

Do not answer any leading questions.
You should say nothing about what you may or may not have done.

As a general rule, and unless otherwise directed, you should remain in your vehicle with your hands in plain sight. This will help put the officer at ease. And believe me, that can mean the difference between a warning and a citation.

ROADSIDE MANNER
(Avoiding a Tense Situation)

The officer has no idea why you committed your alleged traffic violation. You know you are an honest, law-abiding person but unfortunately not everyone is. In 1981, 12 police officers in the United States were murdered while stopping alleged traffic violators.

In Tennessee on April 4, 1981, at approximately 11:15, a police officer was shot and killed after he radioed that he was stopping a speeding vehicle. Unknown to the veteran police officer, the two occupants had robbed a fast food restaurant at gun point. Thinking he had stopped a speeder, the officer approached two armed and desperate felons.

Texas — Separate traffic stops on September 29, 1981 resulted in the deaths of two officers. At approximately 10:45 p.m., a state trooper patrolling his assigned area stopped a motorist for an apparent traffic violation. This trooper, a 13 year veteran, was found dead from a gunshot in the back of the head.

Approximately six miles away, a police officer reportedly stopped the same person for a traffic violation. The driver pulled his vehicle to the side of the road, got out, and walked toward the patrolman. This officer also died, unaware the trooper had been gunned down minutes before.

Pennsylvania — A police officer with a major city in Pennsylvania, stopped a vehicle being driven in the wrong direction on a city street. This officer was shot and killed at approximately 4:00 a.m., on December 9, 1981, apparently as he was questioning the driver.

Mississippi — At approximately 2:00 p.m., on December 31, 1981, a veteran highway patrol officer was killed after making a routine traffic stop. He reportedly was stabbed by four occupants of a vehicle who then seized his .357 handgun and shot him in the head. The suspects were then apprehended in a stolen vehicle.

Kansas — At approximately 8:00 p.m., on July 11, 1981, a veteran trooper was slain as he approached a vehicle he had stopped for speeding. Reportedly, he was shot in the neck and chest with a .357 magnum handgun. The driver then took the officer's service revolver and fled the area. However, two motorists arriving on the scene observed the murderer's vehicle leaving and relayed a description. The driver was later captured and arrested.

As you can imagine, law officers seldom have an idea why the car or vehicle they stopped committed the alleged traffic violation.

Don't be irritated with the officer for trying to stay alive. Think about how to conduct yourself when stopped by the police. The best advice is to let the officer approach you, and keep your hands where he can see them. A good place is on the steering wheel.

If you don't carry your wallet in your back pocket, it's not a good idea to place it in the glove compartment or under the seat. If you are stopped, reaching in these areas is just asking for tension.

When traveling, a good place to put your wallet is on the dash or on the visor. Then, if you're stopped, the officer can readily see exactly what you're reaching for.

This of course does not guarantee a warning ticket instead of a citation, but it can't hurt.

SHOULD I TRY TO TALK MY WAY OUT OF A TICKET?

If you have a bonafide emergency, by all means explain this to the officer who stopped you.

A better way to handle the situation is to call before leaving for the emergency. Dial 911 or some other emergency number and explain the nature of your situation. Provide the proper agency with your name, nature of your emergency, direction of travel (route), vehicle description, license number, when you will be leaving, and where you are going. It's also good to add why you couldn't wait for an ambulance or other emergency equipment.

If you can't call or simply forgot to tell the officer, it's no guarantee against a citation; but if your emergency is bonafide, you will have a very strong defense.

Most states have a reasonable and prudent speed law. This means, is speed reasonable and/or prudent under the existing laws? However, don't mention being late for work or a date. By all means, don't tell the officer you are in a hurry. "So could you please speed things up?"

SHOULD I TRY TO INTIMIDATE THE OFFICER?

Attempt that out on the streets and I can just about guarantee you a citation.

You will also stand out in the officer's mind.

The officer is not going to "try" the case on the street. That is the job of a judge and a jury.

SHOULD I DEMAND TO SEE THE RADAR READING, THE RADAR UNIT, OR VASCAR?

You can ask - that would be more tactful than to demand. However, in some jurisdictions the officer is not required to "lock in" or freeze a reading. There may be nothing to see, and that's not unusual. If, for instance, you were clocked on a speedometer or stop watch, there would be nothing to see. I suggest you politely ask what the brand name of the radar is and after you have received your citation, write down the brand name for future reference.

SHOULD I ASK THE OFFICER IF HE IS QUALIFIED TO OPERATE THE RADAR OR VASCAR?

The street is no place for that question. A court of law is where that type of question comes up.

About the only thing you will accomplish by asking the officer about his skill in using the radar or vascar is to alienate the officer, drawing attention to yourself.

WHAT'S TAKING SO LONG?

"Hey, officer, what's taking so long in writing that ticket? See here, I'm in a hurry.

"What's the matter? Are you a rookie?

"Can't you write any faster than that?"

Any reader who has been stopped, and waited as the officer took time writing the citation or warning most likely wondered what on earth was taking so long. But if you understand the officer's point of view, you won't become so irritated and eventually draw attention to yourself with your negative attitude and turn a warning into a citation.

There are several common reasons why the citation seems to take so long:

1. DRIVER FORGOT HIS/HER DRIVER'S LICENSE

You would be surprised at the number of persons whose licenses are suspended or revoked and continue to drive. Most of these persons had to surrender their licenses to the state. Naturally, they do not have licenses to show the officer.

The only way the officer can verify that you are not under suspension is to check with your state's Department of Motor Vehicles through a computer called *law enforcement teletype system*. The delay in obtaining information is directly proportional to the number of requests for information. These requests are taken in the order in which they are received. Therefore, if there were fifty requests for information ahead of the officer who stopped you, he would have to wait some time for his answer about you or your vehicle.

Remember, it was you who didn't have your license with you.

2. DRIVER DOES NOT HAVE THE REGISTRATION OR PROOF OF OWNERSHIP FOR THE CAR HE/SHE IS DRIVING.

As with the driver's license, most states require a certificate, sometimes called the registration. This must be carried in the vehicle so positive proof of ownership may be established. This, however, is not the title. The title should *NEVER* be carried in the vehicle. (If stolen, the vehicle could be sold if the title were inside.) If you do not have your registration certificate or similar document issued by your state department of Motor Vehicles or county treasurer's office, obtain a copy from one of these agencies.

The officer has no way of knowing whether or not you should have the vehicle. When doubt exists the officer will check with the NCIC (National Crime Information Center) located in Washington, D.C., to determine if the vehicle is stolen.

He will also check with the state where the license plates were issued to determine the proper owner's name and address. He will also check to determine if the license plates really belong on the vehicle to which they are attached.

As with the license check, this may take time. That may explain the delay.

3. CHECKING FOR A WANTED PERSON.

Many drivers who are issued citations to appear in court never show up. The judge, after the date the driver was required to appear in court, will issue a bench warrant.

This warrant commands any law enforcement officer to arrest this person and hold him so he can be brought before the court, to answer not only to the original charge but additional charges of failure to appear.

CHAPTER FIVE
PREPARING YOURSELF FOR COURT
(Without an Attorney)

I got a ticket and I am mad, madder than hell. Mad at myself, mad at the cop, mad at the world in general. All I want to do is get on down the road. Sound familiar?

That's probably the worst attitude in the world to have at the time. If you find yourself cited for any violation, you should think back to these words: Calm, collected and I need some information written down right now.

Be a professional at defending your license and billfold. Take a sheet of paper (don't ever trust your memory). What is recorded on this sheet of paper depends upon the violation with which you are charged. The key is recording accurate and complete information. All violations require certain basic information. The information common to all violations that you should record is as follows:

- Date of the alleged violation.
- Time of the alleged violation.
- Location of the alleged violation.
- Weather conditions.
- Traffic conditions: Was the traffic heavy or light and were you keeping with the normal flow of traffic.

Specific information about specific violations should also be recorded. Let's examine some common violations and what information should be recorded by you for later use in court.

Speeding. (It does not matter if it is radar, car clock, vascar or aircraft. The information you need is the same.)

- Were you passing another car?
- Were you being passed?
- Were you keeping with the flow of traffic?
- Were the speed limit signs in place?
- What cross traffic was present?
- Were signs warning of radar enforcement in place? (NOTE: Some jurisdictions do not require the placement of warning signs but note them anyway.)
- Could you have seen the warning or speed limit signs as they were placed?
- Were these signs obstructed by parked cars, bushes, etc.?
- Could you have seen them from where you first entered the roadway?

- What kind of location were you ticketed in? Business? Residential? School? County Road? State Highway? Interstate? Special area? Hospital, etc.?
- Who, besides yourself, was in the car?
- What did they see pertaining to the above questions?
- What specifically did the officer say to you?
- What specifically did you or your passengers say to the officer?

NOTE: It is very important to never admit guilt. You don't have to. The laws of our land guarantee that right. Don't answer a leading question, such as, "Do you know why I have stopped you?" The officer knows or should know very well why you were stopped. If he doesn't, it's a "fishing trip."

STOP SIGNS

The same basic questions answered by you and written down apply here but you should add relevant information pertaining to stop signs or in some cases modify the information.
- Was the sign in place?
- Was it hidden by bushes?
- Was it hidden by trees?
- Were there parked cars, vans, busses, etc., in the area obscuring the sign?

NOTE: If the reason you could not see the sign was because it was blocked by a parked car, write down the license number for later use in court. Don't overlook the description of the car and exactly how it was blocking your view of the stop sign. Don't forget photos.

If the sign was hidden by bushes, trees or any other obstacle, photograph it. Pictures look great in court.

DRIVING LEFT OF CENTER

This is a common violation and will usually result in your being stopped, not so much for the violation, but to determine if you have had too much to drink. Keeping yourself under control will usually be rewarded with a warning, unless you are too drunk to legally drive.

Let's say that the officer who stopped you for driving left of center is strictly enforcing that statute. What should you look for to make notes?
- Were the No Passing signs properly in place?
- Could you have seen them?

— 27 —

- Did you, from where you entered the roadway, have adequate notice you were in a no passing zone?
- Was the yellow "no passing" paint stripe present?
- Was the paint stripe so badly faded that you could not see it?
- Did rain or the sun or the street lights obscure the no passing zone lines? If so, you could not have reasonably seen the stripe on the road. Record that fact and photograph it, if possible. Look over the location of the alleged violation very carefully, on the same day as the violation. Don't delay. The more information you can gather at the scene of the violation, the stronger your defense will be in court.

FOLLOWING TOO CLOSE

Generally speaking, this type of violation will only be enforced in the event of an accident, where one car slams into the rear of another. Occasionally an officer will issue a citation for this violation even though an accident did not happen. What should you then look for in the way of clues for your defense?

- How much room existed between your car and the car you were following?
- What was your speed?
- What were the present traffic conditions like: Heavy? Light? Etc.?
- What was the road condition like? Clear? Icy? Snowy? Sandy? Pot-holed?
- Was the car you were following slowing down?
- Did the car you were following have a turn indicator activated?
- Was the car you were following slamming on its brakes?
- Did a car squeeze between you and the car you were following?
- What kind of vehicle were you following?

RED LIGHTS, TURN ARROWS, NO TURN SIGNS

- Were these signs in place and operating properly?
- What was your EXACT position when the light turned red, arrow went off, etc.?

By now you should have a fairly good idea of what information you should record. I am equally certain some of you will think of other important bits of information that pertain to your specific case. The key to a good defense is information, documentation and photographs.

If you can convince the court that you know what you are

doing and can show that the officer made an error, a reasonable doubt may exist. And that is all you need to obtain a not guilty verdict—REASONABLE DOUBT.

Remember this: Information available today is gone forever tomorrow.

Keep a clear head and protect your license to drive and hard earned money.

I also strongly recommend you take the time and go to Traffic Court in a place convenient for you. These proceedings are open to the public. Call or go to the court and check the agenda for several cases similar to yours. Attend the proceeding. See the SYSTEM in action. If you follow my advice you will be far better prepared to defend yourself when the time comes.

I am confident your eyes will be opened, and you will see the value of your preparation.

THE OFFICER PREPARING FOR TRIAL

The officer, like you, has made notes about the violation. He will use these notes to refresh his memory of the facts about the citation he issued to you. Believe it or not, you have the advantage over the officer.

Bet you do. The officer has contacted many people and most likely written many citations. Since he doesn't know who will contest a citation and who won't, his memory of the citation by trial time may be a little vaque.

Your memory along with your notes may be the difference.

Do not under any circumstances attract attention to yourself by becoming argumentative or "Standing out" in the officer's mind.

— 29 —

Most officers will not lie about what happened and will tell the truth to the best of their ability. And while it is true most officers are professional, they are not flawless. Neither is the equipment that they use.

I am reminded of a rookie police officer I knew. He was fresh from the police academy and ready to go, full of laws and procedures. One afternoon he checked out his police cruiser and proceeded to patrol his assigned area. The speedometer in his patrol car was acting up a little bit, bouncing between 40 m.p.h. and 60 m.p.h.

"No problem," he thought. "It's certified and I can estimate," he resolved.

Using that logic, he stopped and issued a citation to a driver for speeding 40 m.p.h. in a 25 m.p.h. zone. All the while the police car speedometer was bouncing wildly from 60 to 40. The rookie never gave one second thought to his huge error.

The cited driver (thank God) contested the citation.

The officer testified truthfully about the speedometer. The case was promptly dismissed. The officer was sharply spoken to by the judge for bringing that sort of case into his court.

Would justice have been served if this innocent person had not taken his case to court? My answer is no.

I was that rookie police officer.

I have never made that mistake again.

WHAT DOES THE PROSECUTOR HAVE TO PROVE?

In the back of this book you will find a section called the Defendant's guide to the prosecutor's case.

In that section you will find check lists for various traffic offenses. These are your guidelines to the case the prosecutor must prove to the court beyond a reasonable doubt.

It lists the elements the prosecutor must bring forth and admit as evidence before a judge or jury.

The prosecutor must in all trial situations establish a case beyond the point where a reasonable man would wonder about his fellow man's guilt. Mere suspicion is not sufficient to find a person guilty.

Generally the prosecutor will have to establish certain things in all traffic cases. These are as follows:
 A. Witness background:
  Name
  Length of employment
  Capacity
  Training
 B. Details of the alleged violation:
  Where it occured
  When it occured
  How it occured
  Type and description of vehicle
  Identification of the driver as defendant
  Maintaining contact with suspect vehicle
  Other events about the alleged violation
 C. Proper use of special equipment if used:
  Radar
  Vascar
  Speedometer in patrol unit
  Stop watch

INITIAL APPEARANCE

When the officer issued you a citation he also gave you a court date. It is on this date you will appear in court and enter your initial plea. This plea may be one of three acceptable pleas.
 Not guilty
 Guilty
 Nolo contendere (No Contest)

Guilty and nolo contendere are really one and the same. It means you pay a fine and have the prescribed number of points taken away from your license. Don't let anyone tell you differently.

If you plead not guilty, the judge will set a date for trial. You will be required to appear in court on that date.

CONTINUANCE

If, for some reason, you will be unable to appear at your initial appearance or trial date you have the right to ask for a continuance.

The reasons for granting a continuance vary. I have prepared a partial list of generally accepted reasons: Illness (Yours or that of a very close relative); death in the family; bonafide business reason;

collection of evidence not yet available; your witness will not be available (you can have the court subpoena your witness to compel his attendance); and personal religious holiday.

NOTE: Remember if you do not contact the court and ask for a continuance or the continuance is not granted and you fail to appear in court on the day you were set to appear, a warrant for your arrest will be issued. That means you can be jailed and required to post a money bond to secure your release from custody.

This can be very expensive.

For example, you failed to appear in traffic court and a warrant was issued for your arrest. For the sake of argument, let's say you were stopped and a police officer checked you for being wanted 400 miles from where you were to appear in court. In most cases, you would be arrested and jailed. A bond would be required before you would be released from custody. If you could not post the bond, the Sheriff's Department or similiar agency would be sent to pick you up where you are jailed and return you to the court that issued the warrant. You would pay the transportation cost and the warrant service cost. You would pay these even if you were innocent of the original violation. It is a crime not to appear on a citation.

TRIAL DATE

This is it! This is the adversary system of justice put to the test. This is the day set forth by the judge for the facts of the case to be brought forward in open court.

You prepared yourself for court by making good notes. You took my advice and attended several similar cases in open court and have a basic idea of what to expect.

I also strongly suggest you go to the public library in the state you are charged, look up the statute and copy it. Break the statute down into the elements the prosecutor must prove and take this to court with you. I have reproduced several statutes as you would find them in a law

book and broken them down (removed legal 'mumbo jumbo') into the elements the state must prove to receive a conviction. While it would be impossible for me to describe for you every possible aspect of what could happen in court, I will give you

some pointers on what to expect in the proceedings. I have also provided in the back of the book a guide to the prosecutor's case. You are your own key to a successful defense.

BASIC SPEED RULES

BREAKDOWN OF ELEMENTS:
No person / drive / vehicle / highway / speed / greater reasonable / prudent / conditions / hazards / person / drive / safe / appropriate / speed / intersection / railroad crossing / curve / hill crest / narrow / winding / roadway / weather / highway conditions / special hazard exists / requires / lower speed.

MAXIMUM LEGAL LIMITS:
    Residential 25 m.p.h.
    Business 25 m.p.h.
    Freeway 55 m.p.h.
    Dustless highway 55 m.p.h.
    Not dustless highway 50 m.p.h. (not state highway)

    Maximum limits / may / alter / for cause / lower.
    Department roads / local authority / shall / erect / suitable / signs / notice / to motorists.

Duty upon approaching stop sign -
    Every person operating a motor vehicle shall upon approaching any stop sign erected in accordance with section 424.01, cause such vehicle to come to a complete stop with front wheels parallel with the stop sign.

BREAKDOWN OF ELEMENTS
    Person / operating / vehicle / shall / approach / stop sign / legally erected / stop / vehicle / front wheels / next / to / stop sign.

THE JUDGE'S OPENING REMARKS
(Your Day In Court)

When the Judge enters the courtroom, every person in the court is expected to rise. It's a matter of courtesy that should not be neglected. The judge will then read the formal complaint and ask you if you are ready to proceed to trial or if you wish to change your plea to guilty.

The judge, assuming you stuck to your plea of not guilty, will then ask if you are represented by an attorney or if you are representing yourself.

Since it's a minor traffic offense, you are representing yourself. The judge will then ask the prosecutor if he is ready to proceed. Assuming he is, the trial will begin.

This basic guide will cover most traffic trial situations.

I. Opening Statements
(Occasionally these statements are waived.)

A. The prosecutor will make a brief statement of what he intends to prove during the trial.

B. The defendant makes a statement about what he intends to show and on what he hopes to cast doubt.

C. Unless you are well-versed in courtroom procedure it is best you waive an opening statement.

II. Motion to Amend a Citation (Ticket)

A. This occurs when the officer or prosecutor realizes an error was made in how the ticket was written.

B. Some of these errors are grave. Some are relatively petty.

C. Examples of errors law enforcement officers make in the issuance of citations:
   1. Statute Number
      (a) The statute number does not agree with the written charge (or vice versa).
   2. Date of violation
   3. Time of violation
   4. Location where violation occurred
   5. Driver description
   6. Type of vehicle

Special Note: I have been in situations where the citation was faulty or some error existed. Each time this occurred, the prosecution, *especially* if the person was representing himself, asked for amendment of the complaint or citation. Each time, the Judge presiding over the proceeding asked the defendant (you) if there was any objection.

— 34 —

You bet you object. Even if the trial judge allows the amendment it's on record that you objected. Why object? What's your basis for objection? Simply, if the officer made an error in the complaint, what other errors did he make?

Was he so preoccupied with other matters that he was uncertain with his facts?

See what I mean? You are trying to cast doubt upon the officer's facts.

The State's Case
III. (Direct Testimony)

A. The state will present its case first.

B. A state's witness will be called by the prosecutor and sworn in by the judge, bailiff, or clerk.

C. The prosecutor will then ask the witness questions about the charge against you. Using the guide in the back of this book, make notes about the witness' testimony. You will use this in cross-examination.

IV. Cross-Examination

A. When the prosecutor has finished asking a witness questions, you may ask the witness questions about what he said.

B. *You do not* testify or give your side of the case at this point.

C. It is your goal to impeach the witness. That is, show the court the witness' testimony is faulty (casting a shadow of doubt).

D. You will have the opportunity to cross-examine each witness the state calls.

E. Remember you don't testify at this point.

F. Make notes of what each witness testifies for cross examination.

V. Re-Direct Testimony

Since the burden of proof lies with the state, the prosecutor is allowed to ask each witness you cross-examine additional questions. This is done in an attempt to clarify or remove any shadows you, in cross-examination, have cast.

VI. Your Motion For A Directed Verdict of Not Guilty

If you feel the prosecutor has failed to prove the case against you beyond a reasonable doubt you may ask the court for a directed verdict of not guilty. You must state your reasons for believing the state failed to prove its case. Reasons for a directed verdict of "not guilty" include:

1. Prosecutor failed to show or establish a prima facie case against you
2. Prosecutor failed to establish Jurisdiction (where the offense happened)
3. Officer failed to identify the driver
4. Officer failed to identify the vehicle
5. Officer failed to show the equipment was operating properly, equipment such as: radar, vascar, speedometer, stopwatch, etc.
6. Prosecutor failed to prove the elements of the offense
7. Failed to show location of equipment and that equipment was working properly.
8. Failed to establish time
9. Officer failed to identify himself (uniform, badge or I.D. card).

NOTE: Some jurisdictions require a police officer to display his badge to the person whom he intends to arrest or cite. Other jurisdictions do not require this. Before you attempt to use this as a basis for a directed verdict of not guilty, check the laws or call a police agency and ask what the law is.

VII. Prosecutor Failed to Establish Foundation for Testimony.

Without **judicial notice** or supporting testimony, the prosecutor cannot claim that a person is qualified to operate a piece of equipment. He must first establish, through testimony, that the person who is being questioned is qualified to give such testimony.

NOTE: Don't be alarmed if the judge denies this motion. Unless the judge is convinced the prosecutor has made a grave error and the facts of the case indicate the witness has made errors, the judge will most likely deny your motion. But . . . it's worth a try.

DEFENDANT'S CASE
VIII. Your Turn to Testify

A. Before you testify be sure you understand: You have the right to remain silent, and anything you say can and will be used against you.

NOTE: I have sat in on or been a witness at hundreds of traffic trials. I have listened to dozens of well meaning persons (just like you) go into court, take the stand and proceed to convict themselves.

B. **Hanging yourself on the stand (Examples of the executioner's axe):**
Speeding: "I might have been going 35 in that 25 zone but I sure wasn't going 40."

"I couldn't have been speeding. My car won't go that fast . . . usually."

(Stop Sign Violation)
1. "I slowed down and looked both ways before I drove past that stop sign."
2. "I saw the officer, so how could I have not stopped for the stop sign?"

(Left of Center Violation)
1. "If I was driving left of the center line, I would have hit someone."
2. "It's possible my left tire touched the line, but only for a second."

(Following Too Close)
1. "The vehicle in front of me was traveling much too slow. I wanted to hurry it up."
2. "The vehicle in front of me slammed on its brakes to avoid a dog, so I hit him. I couldn't help it."

(No Driver's License on Your Person)
1. "I left my license home."
2. "I lost my license along with my wallet two months ago."

NOTE: I think you get the picture. Watch what you say on the stand. Don't by your own testimony prove the prosecution's case against you.

WHAT SHOULD YOU DO ON THE WITNESS STAND?

Remember you have the right to remain silent. If you do testify, anything you testify to can be used against you. Do your homework and know what you are saying. Remember, anything you testify to can be challenged by the prosecutor. Don't convict yourself by admitting any guilt.

RESTING YOUR CASE
After you have finished testifying and the prosecutor is finished with his cross-examination, you rest your case with the court.

RECALLING A WITNESS
The prosecutor has the right to recall a witness to rebut any testimony or doubt you may have cast upon the case. You have the right to cross-examine the witness.

CLOSING ARGUMENTS
At this point the prosecution will sum up what has been testified. That is, he will list the facts of his case.

THE VERDICT

Once both sides have rested their cases, it is up to the judge to determine if the state has proved its case against you. As we have discussed, in the American system of justice, the burden of proof rests with the prosecutor.

If the judge returns a not guilty verdict, the charges are dismissed. If on the other hand the judge returns a guilty verdict, a fine is imposed, court costs are assessed and points are ordered removed from your license.

MOST IMPORTANT NOTE: What can I do if I'm found guilty? If you have been found guilty there are two things you can do. Ask for a new trial with the next higher court, or ask for probation.

I NEW TRIAL

Here an appeals judge will either "hear" the case again and rule on the evidence, or he will review a transcript of the first trial. A transcript is a written record of exactly what was testified to in court. It also includes any orders by the trial judge.

The appeals judge, depending on how he chooses to handle the appeal, will review the transcript for errors in points of law. He will then either affirm the conviction or reverse the decision of the trial judge.

If the appeals judge chooses to hear the case again, the proceedings will be much the same as in your first trial, but with a new judge presiding.

II PROBATION

A very little known fact is that you have the right to ask the court for probation. Probation, if granted, is not as terrible as it sounds. It can save you hundreds of dollars on your insurance premiums.

If the trial judge grants you probation, the record of your conviction may never leave the confines of the trial court.

Oh, yes! You pay your fine and court costs.

As an added bonus, the points normally against your license are not taken from you, provided you abide by the terms of your probation.

Such terms can vary but generally will include:

No conviction of any violation of the law.

Full payment of any fines or court costs.

The length of your probation depends solely on the trial judge who heard the case.

I have known probation periods to last from 3 months to 1 year depending on the circumstances.

If the judge grants you probation, be very careful how you drive during the period of your probation.

Slipping can be very expensive. All points will be assessed as well as new points for the additional violation.

IT'S YOUR LICENSE — PROTECT IT!

SUMMARY

By now it should be clear. The protection of your license and hard earned money is a serious business. The job of the prosecutor is to convince the judge that you are guilty. It is your job to show the judge a reasonable doubt exists about your guilt.

Only by gathering information and presenting it properly to the court can you hope to be found not guilty. Your right to have your day in court is absolute. Use that right or one day you may lose it.

IN THIS ROOM JUSTICE IS SERVED, BUT IT'S UP TO YOU TO USE THAT RIGHT.

CHAPTER SIX
DEFENDANT'S GUIDE TO THE PROSECUTOR'S CASE

In all trial situations, the prosecutor is faced with the responsibility of establishing an adequate foundation for the introduction of evidence. In using the outlines, two considerations should be kept in mind. First, the outlines do not represent the fullest, or the least, extent of questioning used by prosecutors to introduce matters into evidence.

Second, foundational requirements will vary in any jurisdiction depending on the individual preferences of the trial court.

The following outlines are designed for you to take into court to assist you in properly defending yourself.

HOW TO USE THIS GUIDE

This guide is designed for you to take into court. It is by no means the complete case the prosecutor could use against you. It is a basic guide to what the prosecutor would usually have to prove to earn a conviction.

This guide is designed so you can photocopy the violation that pertains to your situation and take it to court with you on your trial date.

Use the note section of this guide for your notes about the answers to the questions by the witness. You should also take a pad of paper in case a question is asked that I have not listed.

If you find yourself charged with a violation that does not appear in this guide, study the questions as listed in all the various violation outlines I have provided for you. Select the questions that pertain and follow the format you feel best fits your situation.

PHYSICAL EVIDENCE
(Chain of Custody)

The introduction of Physical Evidence in minor traffic offenses is rare. However, the chance of its introduction does exist. Therefore I will briefly cover the requirements to insure proper entry of this evidence either by you as the Defendant or by the Prosecutor for the state.

The most important consideration of Physical Evidence is chain of custody.

Chain of Custody is a complete list of who had control of the evidence from the moment it was found until it was introduced in court as an exhibit.

A prescribed foundation must be followed to insure the proper introduction of Physical Evidence.

QUESTIONS	NOTES:
Witness Background (Qualification to Present Evidence).	
Name.	
Employment.	
Length of Employment.	
Mark Exhibit (not necessary if pre-marked prior to trial) for identification.	
Exhibit Inquiry.	
Identifying feature(s) of exhibit - recognition of exhibit.	
Identifying marks which assist in identification. Time and circumstances of placement of identifying marks on exhibit.	
Inquiry as to initial circumstance when witness became familiar with exhibit.	
Chain of custody of exhibit from witness to others.	

QUESTIONS:	NOTES:
Circumstances of recent identification of exhibit by witness (how it has returned to possession of witness).	
Circumstances of present condition of exhibit when first seen by witness (condition substantially the same).	
Offering of exhibit into evidence (subject to relevancy or other objection).	

SPEEDING
(Mobile Radar)

Generally speaking, the officer who issued you the ticket will be the Prosecutor's only witness. This outline deals with alleged speed violations where mobile radar was used.

SECTION ONE

Witness Background	
QUESTIONS:	NOTES:
Name.	
Length of employment.	
Was witness so employed on the date of alleged violation?	
Was witness on duty?	
Did witness display authority to issue citation, badge, identification card, etc.?	
OPERATION OF MOBILE RADAR (Generally)	
Explanation of mobile radar.	
Does witness understand how to properly set up, calibrate and use radar?	
Education and training in operation of mobile radar units.	
Properly certified in operations of radar unit by the manufacturer.	
Certification to operate mobile radar on the date of the violation.	
Length of certification by witness.	
OPERATION OF MOBILE RADAR (With reference to offense)	
Date of violation.	
Time of violation.	

QUESTIONS:	NOTES:
Location of violation.	
Witness location on observing alleged violation.	
Obstructions to clear view of violation site.	
Identification of vehicle.	
Direction of travel of vehicle.	
Direction of travel of witness vehicle.	
Reason police attention was drawn to defendant vehicle.	
Was the mobile radar operational at the time of the sighting?	
Was the police car being operated at a steady speed?	
Was a speed reading obtained on the radar reading module?	
How long was defendant vehicle tracked by the radar?	
What was the distance between witness' vehicle and radar vehicle?	
Objects in the area that might have affected the reading.	
Statement of radar reading obtained by the officer.	

SUBSEQUENT EVENTS TO OBTAINING READING:

Maintain visual contact with vehicle.	
Contact with operator, passengers.	
Identification of defendant as operator of vehicle.	
Relation of conversations conducted between witness and defendant and/or passengers.	
Issuance of citation.	

QUESTIONS:	NOTES:
ACCURACY OF MOBILE RADAR UNIT:	
Officer trained in testing procedure of technique in determining accuracy of unit.	
Narrative as to technique.	
Employment of technique by witness.	
Independent testing of unit.	
WHEN TESTED	
By whom tested.	
Testing or calibration and use of technique mentioned above.	
Unit operating accurately at time of testing.	
Subsequent testing of unit on date of offense.	
Posted speed limit in area of offense.	
Venue.	

SPEED (Vascar)

Vascar is not radar. Vascar is a device designed to calculate time vs. distance and compute that to speed.

QUESTIONS:	NOTES:
Witness Background:	
Name.	
Employment.	
Length of Employment.	
Employment on date of offense.	
Rank.	
Shift.	
Shift duties (area of patrol and type of unit being operated by witness — Vascar).	

OPERATION OF VASCAR (generally)

Explanation of Vascar.	
How long operating Vascar unit?	
Education and training in operation of Vascar unit.	
Certification to operate Vascar on date of offense.	

OPERATION OF VASCAR (with reference to offense):

Time, date and location of first observation of defendant's vehicle, including identification of vehicle.	
Direction of travel of above vehicle.	
Direction of travel of witness' vehicle.	

QUESTIONS:	NOTES:
Reason for drawing witness' attention to defendant's vehicle.	
Vascar unit operational at time of sighting.	
Obtaining of clocking of defendant's vehicle with Vascar.	
Type of clocking obtained.	
Stationary.	
Following.	
Approaching.	
Angle.	
Procedure used to obtain particular type of clocking. Narrative on how Vascar computes into speed.	
Assurance that procedures generally used to secure particular type of clocking were used in this instance.	
Distance over which clocking was made.	
Result obtained from clocking.	

QUESTIONS:	NOTES:
SUBSEQUENT EVENTS (after obtaining clocking):	
Maintain visual contact with vehicle.	
Contact with operator, passengers.	
Identification of defendant as operator of vehicle clocked.	
Relation of conversations conducted between witness and defendant and/or passengers.	
Issuance of citation.	
ACCURACY OF VASCAR UNIT:	
Unit checked for accuracy on date of offense.	
When tested.	
By whom tested.	
Calibration of unit.	
Measurement by witness of calibrated distance.	
Independent testing of unit for accuracy by witness. Subsequent testing of unit on date of offense.	
POSTED SPEED LIMIT IN AREA OF OFFENSE	
Venue.	

SPEED
(Aircraft Clock)

QUESTIONS: NOTES:

Officer in Aircraft	
Name.	
Employment.	
Length of Employment.	
Employment on date of offense.	
Rank.	
Shift.	
Shift duties (area of patrol and type of unit being operated by witness-aircraft speed detection).	

OPERATION BY AIRCRAFT
SPEED DETECTION GENERALLY

Education and training.	
Where training was received.	
When training occurred.	
Type of training obtained (techniques).	

TRAINING IN TECHNIQUE TO INSURE ACCURACY

Narrative on technique.

SPEED DETECTION BY AIRCRAFT

Types.	
How often?	
Local, regional or national programs of training?	

CERTIFICATION:

Certification on date of offense.	
Recertification, if any.	

OPERATION OF AIRCRAFT SPEED DETECTION WITH REFERENCE TO OFFENSE:

Time, date and location of aircraft speed detection units.	
Assurance that unit was operating accurately at time of use.	
Narrative on technique used to insure accuracy.	
Accuracy insured approximately how long before its use with respect to this offense.	
Initial observation of defendant's vehicle.	

SPEED DETECTION BY AIRCRAFT (continued)
INITIAL OBSERVATION OF DEFENDANT'S VEHICLE

QUESTIONS:	NOTES:
Description of vehicle. Location of vehicle.	
Direction of travel of defendant's vehicle.	
Direction of travel of aircraft.	
Reason for drawing witness' attention to defendant's vehicle.	
Timing of vehicle over a given distance.	
Determination of distance. Location of distance. Layout which was used.	
Familiarity with distance lay-out.	
Additional clockings which were made (if any).	

SECURING OF TIMING OF VEHICLE OVER ONE MILE LAY-OUT:

Timing secured.	
Computation of timing into average speed over one mile.	
Comparison of time to distance with respect to computation chart.	
Radio description of vehicle upon which speed was secured to ground unit.	
Maintenance of visual contact with vehicle upon which clocking was obtained.	

SPEED DETECTION BY AIRCRAFT (continued)

QUESTIONS:	NOTES:
Observance of ground officer stopping clocked vehicle.	
Confirmation that clocked vehicle same as that stopped by ground officer.	
Posted speed limit in area of offense.	

OFFICER ON GROUND:

Witness Background:

Name.	
Employment.	
Length of Employment.	
Employment on date of offense.	
Rank.	
Shift.	
Shift duties.	
Aircraft speed detection in conjunction with aircraft officer.	
Operating ground mobile unit.	
General location of aircraft unit.	

SPEED DETECTION BY AIRCRAFT (continued)
OPERATION OF UNIT WITH REFERENCE TO OFFENSE:

QUESTIONS:	NOTES:
Time, date and location of first observation of defendant's vehicle including identification of vehicle.	
Direction of travel of above vehicle.	
Direction of travel of witness vehicle (Police vehicle).	
Reason for drawing attention to defendant's vehicle. (Radio call from aircraft unit concerning clocking).	

SUBSEQUENT EVENTS:

Stopping of vehicle.	
Confirmation of stop with aircraft.	
Contact with operator and/or passengers.	
Identification of operator same as defendant.	
Relation of any conversations conducted between witness and defendant and/or passengers.	
Issuance of citation.	
Venue.	

FOLLOWING TOO CLOSE VIOLATIONS

The State must prove you were following another vehicle unreasonably close, creating a hazard.

QUESTIONS:	NOTES:
WITNESS:	
FOLLOWING TOO CLOSE (GENERALLY):	
Weather Conditions.	
Traffic Conditions.	
Road Conditions.	
FOLLOWING TOO CLOSE (SPECIFICALLY):	
Identification Driver.	
Identification Vehicle.	
Description of vehicle being followed too close.	
How long did officer observe violation before action was taken?	
What drew officer's attention to defendant vehicle?	
Location vehicle stopped.	
Conversation with driver.	
Conversation with passenger.	
Venue.	

STOP SIGN VIOLATIONS

The State must prove you failed to come to a complete stop at or near the crosswalk side of the sign.

QUESTIONS:	NOTES:
Witness Background.	
Name.	
Employment.	
Length of employment.	
Duties.	

STOP SIGNS (GENERALLY)

Was sign in place?	
Was sign legible?	
Was sign obscured?	
Was sign "a uniform sign"?	

STOP SIGNS (SPECIFICALLY)

Identification of defendant as driver.	
Description of vehicle defendant was driving.	
Where was defendant vehicle first observed?	
Where was police car?	

QUESTIONS:	NOTES:
What drew officer's attention to vehicle?	
Location vehicle stopped.	
Conversation with driver.	
Conversation with passengers.	
Could defendant have stopped out of sight and been legally stopped?	
Traffic conditions.	
Weather conditions.	
Issue citation.	
Venue.	

RED LIGHT VIOLATIONS

QUESTIONS:	NOTES:
Witness Background.	
Name.	
Employment.	
Length of Employment.	
Duties.	

RED LIGHT (GENERALLY)

Was traffic light in place?	
Was red light functioning properly?	
Was red light "Uniformly placed"?	

RED LIGHT (SPECIFICALLY)

QUESTIONS:	NOTES:
Identification of defendant as driver.	
Description of vehicle defendant was driving.	
Where was defendant vehicle first observed?	
Where was police car?	
What drew officer's attention to vehicle?	
Location vehicle stopped.	
Conversation with driver.	
Conversation with passengers.	
Could defendant have stopped out of sight of police unit and been legally stopped?	
Traffic conditions.	
Weather conditions.	
Issue citation.	
Venue.	

OTHER MINOR VIOLATIONS NOT LISTED:

Remember you should not attempt to defend yourself in a serious traffic offense or any criminal violation with which you have been charged.

Use this question and note section as an outline for violations you are charged with that were not outlined.

QUESTIONS:	NOTES:

QUESTIONS:	NOTES:

GLOSSARY OF LEGAL TERMS

Accident: unforeseen occurrence which results in injury to the person or property of another.

Accuse: To bring formal charge against a person to be heard by a magistrate.

Accuser: Person who makes accusation.

Acquitted: Absolved; found blameless.

Act: To do or perform.

Adjournment: Put off or postpone until another time.

Adjudication: The finding of the court judgement.

Admissable: Referring to those things considered in deciding an issue; things that apply.

Admonition: Reprimand from judge that if action continues, more severe punishment may befall guilty person.

Adversary: An opponent.

Advise: To give opinion.

Affiant: Person who swears to in writing about certain facts making an affidavit.

Affidavit: A written declaration or statement of the facts confirmed by oath.

Affirm: To ratify; make firm.

Affix: To fasten in anyway.

Agenda: List of things to be done.

Agent: One authorized by another to act in his behalf.

Agree: To concur; to settle.

Alcoholic beverage: Beverage that contains alcohol.

Alcoholism: Excessive use of alcoholic beverages.

Allegation: Statement made setting out what the accuser expects to prove.

Allege: To state; recite.

Appeal: To ask a higher court to hear your case and set aside the lower court's verdict.

Appear: To be properly before the court.

Appearance Bond: A set figure demanded (instead of detaining the person) to assure an appearance in court.

Apprehend: To seize; to arrest; to understand.

Attest: State as a fact.

Bail: To secure the release of a person from custody by word or money.

Bail Bond: A document executed by a defendant who has been arrested; to secure release from custody.

Beer: A liquor compounded of malt and hops.

Bench: A seat of judgement or tribunal for the administration of justice.

Bench Warrant: Paper issued by a judge commanding a person be brought before him to answer a charge.

Beyond a Reasonable Doubt: Fully satisfied; entirely convinced; satisfied to a certainty.

Bias: Bent; preconceived idea.

Bill: A formal declaration.

Blind Corner: One where building extends to the property line or is obscuring an intersection.

Car: A vehicle primarily intended for transportation of persons or freight.

Careless: Negligent.

Carriage: A vehicle used especially for the transportation of person in a device drawn by horses, etc.

Casualty: Accident; event due to sudden unexpected acts.

Charge: A formal complaint.

Citation· A writ issued out of a court of competent jurisdiction, commanding a person therein named to appear on a day and do something mentioned.

Cite: To summon; command the presence of a person to answer a charge.

Collide: To strike or dash together.

Collision: Striking together of two objects, one of which may be stationary.

City Court: A court with jurisdiction over a city.

Collision Cause: Reason accident occurred.

Concur: Agree; act together.

Confess: To admit as true.

Contempt of Court: Any act which hinders or obstructs the court in the administration of justice.

Continuance: The adjournment or postponement of an action pending in a court at a later date.

Control: To exercise direct influence over.

Convict: Declare or prove guilty. Compels attendance in court of person wanted there as a witness, including not only the ordinary subpoena, but also a warrant of arrest or attachment if needed.

County Court: A court having jurisdiction over a specific area i.e., a county.

Crime: An act committed or omitted in violation of law forbidding or commanding, upon conviction, punishment.

Cross Examination: The examination of witness at a trial by the party opposed; to test the truthfulness of the witness' story.

Defense: The answer made by a person to a charge.

Demeanor: Attitude and appearance.

Deputy: A person duly authorized by an officer to exercise some or all of the functions pertaining to the office.

Deputy Sheriff (See Deputy).

Discharge: To release.

Due Process of Law: Safeguards set forth in the Constitution; rights of persons presumed innocent until proven guilty by proper legal procedures.

Ear Witness: In the law of evidence, one who attests or can attest to anything as heard by himself.

Ego: I; myself; I such as one.

Emergency: A sudden, unexpected happening of pressing necessity.

Emit: To put forth or send out.

Enforce: To put into effect; to compel obedience.

Enter: To place before the court.

Entrapment: The act of officers or agents of the government inducing a person to commit a crime not contemplated by him; the mere act of an officer in furnishing the accused an opportunity to commit the crime when intent was present is not by itself entrapment.

Entry: The act of making or recording a record.

Establish: To settle or fix firmly.

Evidence: Anything legally presented which proves the charge.

Evidence, Laws of: The aggregate of rules and principles regulating the admissibility, relevancy, weight and sufficiency of evidence in legal proceeding.

Ex Post Facto Law: A law passed after the fact.

Examination: An investigation, search, interrogation.

Excessive Speed: Automobile speed is excessive when beyond driver's control.

Exonerate: To relieve; hold blameless.

Expert Witness: Men of science or possessing special or peculiar knowledge acquired from practical experience.

Fair Hearing: One in which authority is fairly exercised; i.e., due process of law is followed.

Fine: To impose a sum of money as punishment.

Hazard: A risk or peril.

Hazardous: Exposed to or involving danger.

Hearing: Public fact-finding session.

Hearsay: Evidence not proceeding from the personal knowledge of the witness.

Hostile Witness: A witness who is against the side that called him; that party can cross-examine him as though the other side had called him.

Infraction: A breach, violation or infringement of law.

Illegal: Not authorized by law; contrary to law.

Impeach: Challenge; judgement; statement as to impeach the witness.

Implied: Express, not specifically stated, but the meaning is present.

Intent: Design, resolve, or determination with which persons act.

Intersection: Place where two streets or highways come together.

Interstate: Between two or more states.

Interstate Commerce: Traffic, commercial trading, or the transportation of persons or property between or among the several states of the Union or from between points in one state and points in another state.

Interstate Commerce Commission: Composed of eleven persons appointed by the President, empowered to inquire into the business of the carriers affected; to enforce the law to receive, investigate, and determine complaints made to them of any violation of the Acts.

Irrelevant: Does not pertain to.

Jay Walking: Walking diagonally across a street intersection.

Jeopardy Danger: Peril, hazard.

Judge: An officer who presides over legal proceedings.

Judgement: Order of the court.

Judicial Notice: The act by which a court, in conducting a trial, will of its own accord recognize the existence of truth of certain facts having a bearing upon the case.

Jurisdiction: The area of legal right.

Juror: One member of a jury.

Justice: Render every man his due process of law.

Justice of the Peace: A judicial officer of inferior rank, usually has jurisdiction over civil, criminal, and traffic cases.

Knowingly: Consciously; willfully; with intent.

Law judge: A judge who is not learned in the law.

Legal Evidence: A broad term meaning all admissable evidence.

License: Certificate or the document itself which gives permission. Specifically - motor vehicles, "License to operate motor vehicle is mere privilege and not a contract or property right."

License, Streets and Ways: A permit to use street is a mere license revocable at pleasure.

Limit: A restraint; a boundry.

Magistrate: A person clothed with power as a public civil officer.

Mandatory: Containing a command.

Misdemeanor: Offenses lower than felonys; bad conduct.

Muffler: A device used to deaden the noise of escaping gases or vapors from a motor vehicle.

Municipal: Pertaining to a local government.

Neglect: Omit; fail; forebear to do something.

Negligence: The omission to do something which a reasonable man, guided by ordinary circumstances, would do.

Nolo Contendere: "I will not contest"; having the same legal effect as a guilty plea.

Non Judicial Day: A day on which court cannot ordinarily be held and judgement rendered.

Non-resident: One who is not a dweller within jurisdiction in question.

Not Guilty: A plea of contest to the charges; a finding of blamelessness.

Not Guilty by Statute: Directed verdict of not guilty, as state failed to prove its case.

Offender: Person implicated in commission of an offense.

Offense: A crime, misdemeanor or traffic infraction.

Park: Put a vehicle in a place and leave temporarily.

Parking Meter: A device designed to determine the length of time of parking by a vehicle.

Patrolman: A policeman assigned to duty patrolling a certain beat or district.

Peers: Other normal citizens.

Perjury: Willfully lying under oath.

Permit: Allow; consent; let.

Perpetrator: Person who actually commits a crime or offense.

Petition: A written document asking an authority to do something about a wrong; application in writing.

Petty: Small; minor; of less importance.

Plead: Declaration of position, i.e., guilty or not guilty. The utterances of a specific set of circumstances designed to show the judge or jury of innocence.

Points: As used in this book, a system of numbers used to determine when a person should no longer be allowed to retain a license to operate a motor vehicle, because previous behavior indicates a disregard for the law.

Police Court: A court with jurisdiction over minor offenses, i.e., traffic offenses, infractions, etc.

Police Officer: One of a staff of men employed in cities and towns to enforce law.

Preponderance: Greater weight of evidence or evidence which is more credible and convincing to mind.

Prerogative: An exclusive or peculiar privilege.

Presence of an Officer: A violation committed in the presence or view of an officer.

Presumption: Something decided, one way or the other.

Presumption of Innocence: Conclusion drawn by law in favor of one brought to trial; requires acquittal unless guilt is established.

Prima Facie: "At first sight"; on the surface; a fact presumed to be true unless disproved by evidence to the contrary.

Prima Facie Evidence: Evidence good and sufficient to establish a given fact.

Probable Cause: More than mere suspicion; reason to believe; what would lead a reasonable man given a certain set of circumstances.

Prosecutor: The attorney for the state who presents thê case to the court against a person accused of wrongdoing.

Radar: An electronic device that emits a signal used to determine the velocity of a moving object.

Radar Detector: A device used to detect the presence of radar transmitter.

Reasonable: Just; proper; appropriate.

Reasonable and Prudent: Just and proper, using due care as a proper and careful man would do.

Reckless Driving: Operation of automobile in a manner without regard for life or property.

Reciprocity: Mutuality; relation existing between two states granting certain privileges to its own citizens as long as those privileges are afforded to the citizens of the other state.

Registration: An official document denoting ownership and payment of taxes.

Regulate: To fix, establish, or control; to rule.

Reinstate: To reinstall; to re-establish.

Right of Way: The right of passage.

Road Hog: A driver who selfishly occupies the road.

Sheriff: An elected official of a county charged with enforcement of laws in the county.

Speedy Trial: A trial within the reasonable amount of time.

Statute: An act of the legislature, commanding or forbidding certain actions.

Stop: Definite cessation of movement until the way is clear.

Stop Sign: A legally erected and maintained traffic signal requiring traffic to stop before entering into or crossing an intersection.

Subpoena: A legal written order requiring a person to appear or documents to be submitted in court.

Subpoena Duces Tecum: A process by which the court commands a witness who has in his possession or control some document or paper that is pertinent to an issue of a pending controversy.

Summary: Short; concise.

Summon: Require a defendant to appear in court.

Suppress: To put a stop to a thing actually existing; to prohibit.

Suspension: A temporary stop; interruption.

Swear: To put to oath.

Sworn: Verified.

Synopsis: A brief or partial statement.

Thoroughfare: A continuous street.

Ton: A measure of weight.

Traffic: Movement of automobiles from one place to another.

Traffic Regulations: Prescribed rules of conduct to ensure orderly and safe flow of traffic.

Trailer: A separate vehicle, not self-propelled.

Unlawfully: Illegally; wrongfully.

Venue: A neighborhood or county or place in which an act occurred or is declared to have been done; also the geographical division in which an action or prosecution is brought for trial and which is to furnish jurors.

Verdict: Decision of a jury.

Waiver: The intention or voluntary relinquishment of a known right.

Waive: Abandon; throw away.

Warning: A pointing out of danger.

Without prejudice: Not final and can be changed.

Witness: One who being present, personally sees or perceives a thing.

Yield: Relinquish.